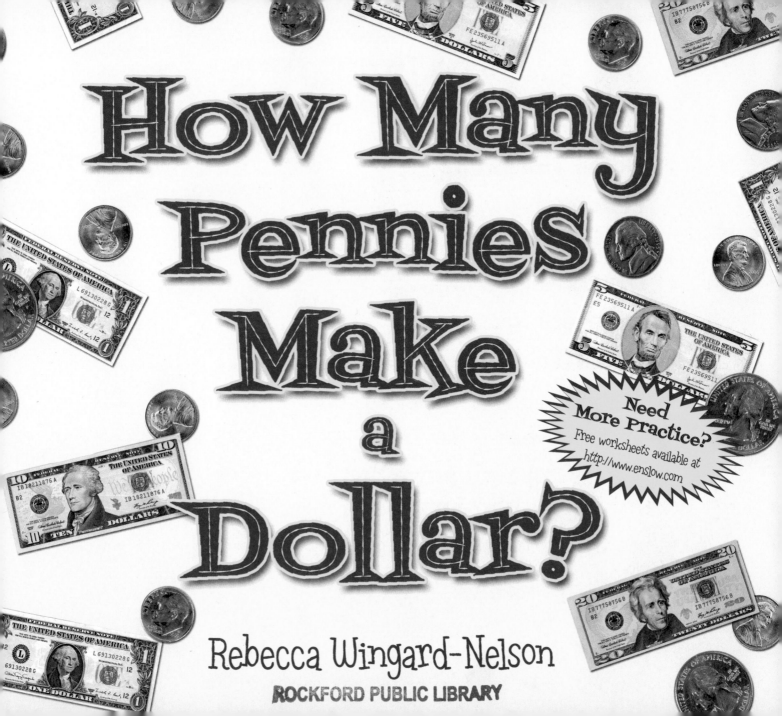

How Many Pennies Make a Dollar?

Need More Practice?
Free worksheets available at
http://www.enslow.com

Rebecca Wingard-Nelson

ROCKFORD PUBLIC LIBRARY

CONTENTS

Coins and Bills

 penny
1¢

 one-dollar bill
$1

 nickel
5¢

 five-dollar bill
$5

 dime
10¢

 ten-dollar bill
$10

 quarter
25¢

 twenty-dollar
bill
$20

3

Pennies

The ¢ symbol means "cents."
One penny = 1¢

You can count pennies to find their total value.

1   2

Two pennies = 2¢

1   2   3   4   5

Five pennies = 5¢

Five pennies equal
one nickel.

5¢   =   5¢

How many pennies equal 10¢?

1   2   3   4   5

6   7   8   9   10

Ten pennies = 10¢

Ten pennies equal one dime.

10¢   =   10¢

How many pennies equal 25¢?

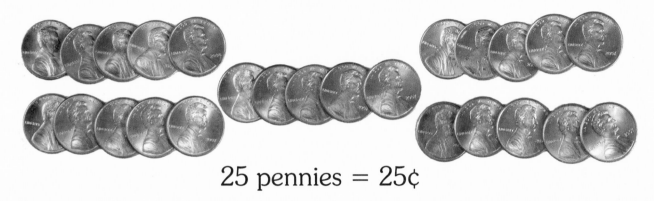

25 pennies = 25¢

Twenty-five pennies equal one quarter.

25¢ = 25¢

Nickels

One nickel = 5¢

You can count nickels by 5s.

| 5 | 10 | 15 | 20 |

Two nickels = 10¢   Three nickels = 15¢   Four nickels = 20¢

How many nickels equal 10¢?
Count by 5s until you reach 10.

5   10

2 nickels = 10¢

Two nickels equal one dime.

10¢   =   10¢

How can you make 10¢ using nickels and pennies together?
Count 5 for a nickel, then 1 more for each penny until you
reach 10.

5   6 7   8   9 10

1 nickel and 5 pennies = 10¢

One nickel and five pennies equal one dime.

10¢   =   10¢

How many nickels equal 25¢?
Count by 5s until you reach 25.

5   10   15   20   25

5 nickels = 25¢

Five nickels equal one quarter.

25¢   =   25¢

Dimes

One dime = 10¢

You can count dimes by 10s.

| 10 | 20 | 30 | 40 | 50 |

Two dimes   = 20¢
Three dimes = 30¢
Four dimes = 40¢
Five dimes   = 50¢

Can you see the pattern?
The number of dimes is the same
as the number in the tens place.
5 dimes = 50¢

What coins are equal to 10¢?

One dime = 10¢

Two nickels = 10¢

 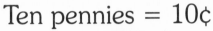

One nickel and
five pennies = 10¢

Ten pennies = 10¢

Quarters

One quarter = 25¢

You can count quarters by 25s.

| 25 | 50 | | 25 | 50 | 75 |

Two quarters = 50¢   Three quarters = 75¢

How can you make 25¢ using dimes and nickels together?

Count 10 for each dime, then 5 more for each nickel until you reach 25.

10   20   25

2 dimes and 1 nickel = 25¢

10   15   20   25

1 dime and 3 nickels = 25¢

25¢

Two dimes and one nickel equal one quarter.

25¢

One dime and three nickels equal one quarter.

Coins That Make a Dollar

Money can be written using a dollar sign and a decimal point. $1.00 means "one dollar." One dollar is equal to 100 cents.

One-dollar bill = 100¢, or $1.00

How many pennies make a dollar?

One hundred pennies = 100¢, or $1.00

How many nickels make a dollar? Count by 5s to 100.

5 10 15 20 25

30 35 40 45 50

55 60 65 70 75

80 85 90 95 100

Twenty nickels = 100¢, or $1.00

How many dimes make a dollar? Count by 10s to 100.

10   20   30   40   50

60   70   80   90   100

Ten dimes = 100¢, or $1.00

How many quarters make a dollar? Count by 25s to 100.

25   50   75   100

Four quarters = 100¢, or $1.00

one-dollar bill = $1.00

4 quarters= $1.00

10 dimes = $1.00

20 nickels = $1.00

100 pennies = $1.00

Bills

A five-dollar bill has the same value as 5 one-dollar bills.

1 five-dollar bill = $5.00   5 one-dollar bills = $5.00

$5.00   = $5.00

A ten-dollar bill has the same value as 10 one-dollar bills.

1 ten-dollar bill = $10.00   10 one-dollar bills = $10.00

$10.00   = $10.00

A ten-dollar bill has the same value as 2 five-dollar bills.

1 ten-dollar bill = $10.00

2 five-dollar bills = $10.00

$10.00 = $10.00

1 twenty-dollar bill = $20.00	2 ten-dollar bills = $20.00	4 five-dollar bills = $20.00	20 one-dollar bills = $20.00

$20.00 $20.00 $20.00 $20.00

LET'S REVIEW

1 nickel = 5¢
5 pennies = 5¢

1 dime = 10¢
2 nickels = 10¢
10 pennies = 10¢

1 quarter = 25¢
5 nickels = 25¢
25 pennies = 25¢

1 one-dollar bill = $1.00
10 dimes = $1.00
20 nickels = $1.00
100 pennies = $1.00

1 five-dollar bill = $5.00
5 one-dollar bills = $5.00

1 ten-dollar bill = $10.00
2 five-dollar bills = $10.00
10 one-dollar bills = $10.00

LEARN MORE

Books

Hill, Mary. *Dollars*. New York: Children's Press, 2005.

Roberson, Erin. *All About Money*. New York: Children's Press, 2004.

Robinson, Elizabeth Keeler. *Making Cents*. Berkeley, Calif.: Tricycle Press, 2008.

Web Sites

H.I.P. Pocket Change.
  <http://www.usmint.gov/kids/>

U.S. Treasury–For Kids.
  <http://www.ustreas.gov/kids/>

INDEX

Enslow Elementary, an imprint of Enslow Publishers, Inc.

Enslow Elementary® is a registered trademark of Enslow Publishers, Inc.

Copyright © 2010 by Enslow Publishers, Inc.

All rights reserved.

No part of this book may be reproduced by any means without the written permission of the publisher.

Library of Congress Cataloging-in-Publication Data

Wingard-Nelson, Rebecca.

   How many pennies make a dollar? / Rebecca Wingard-Nelson.
      p. cm. — (I like money math!)
   Summary: "Introduces young readers to the concept of counting money and the different denominations of money"—Provided by publisher.
   Includes bibliographical references and index.
   ISBN-13: 978-0-7660-3141-8
   ISBN-10: 0-7660-3141-1
   1. Counting—Juvenile literature. 2. Money—Juvenile literature. I. Title.
   QA113.W586 2010
   513.2'11—dc22   2008050052

Printed in the United States of America

10 9 8 7 6 5 4 3 2 1

ISBN-13: 978-0-7660-3656-7 (paperback)
ISBN-10: 0-7660-3656-1 (paperback)

To Our Readers: We have done our best to make sure all Internet Addresses in this book were active and appropriate when we went to press. However, the author and the publisher have no control over and assume no liability for the material available on those Internet sites or on other Web sites they may link to. Any comments or suggestions can be sent by e-mail to comments@enslow.com or to the address on the back cover.

 Enslow Publishers, Inc., is committed to printing our books on recycled paper. The paper in every book contains 10% to 30% post-consumer waste (PCW). The cover board on the outside of each book contains 100% PCW. Our goal is to do our part to help young people and the environment too!

Photo Credits: Shutterstock

Cover Photo: Shutterstock

Enslow Elementary
an imprint of
Enslow Publishers, Inc.
40 Industrial Road
Box 398
Berkeley Heights, NJ 07922
USA

http://www.enslow.com